Sitting quietly
Return to the source
10 years sober
Off the sauce
I recollect a time
I would strive
For just staying alive
Recovery I have been given
This is what it's like
To be living
Going back
I had to start at the beginning
Looking ahead
It's far better than being dead
A job done on the inside
That's what was being said
For the ones starting on there journey
Hold on tight
The path gets rocky
Twists and turns in every direction
The gift of desperation
Once sinking In the mire
A deeper love I have aquired
Spare a thought for the
Still suffering
The disease of addiction
Still to this day
Is quite baffling

Navigation through exploration
Feels brand new
Is this my truth
Articulated
Talking
Eye contact
Body language
I hope I can manage
To hold your gaze
Don't know I am amazed
At what comes my way
Just open my mouth
And say
Thank you for coming
On this day

As I went in a broken man
Didn't understand
God had a plan
Thought I was evil
In my emotions
There were a big upheaval
Didn't think it was real
They was a lot I needed
To conceal
Keep quiet don't squeal
Really is this the deal
Inside in outside
Thinking
Felt like quitting
Instead I got used to sitting
With my thoughts
And my feelings
In my head
At times
I wished to be dead
What happened
Was something
Different instead

For 5 days
I will work and play
Going on holiday
Some might say
It's in his sway
god has blessed
Me for this day
Not so much as sea and sun
Number 1 have fun
Blatant entertainment
Feel so loved
The flame flickers with an ember
The relationships I have with the members
What a pleasure what a privilege
Got the experience
Got the mileage
Feel excited
Like a little kid

Can't control
Slipping down a hole
Don't feel whole
Wow what a way to go
If I gave up
It's not tough
Just give in
Fighting
I know it's not right
Fear at its height
Like a sniper
Locked you in the sights
Man down
In this town
Took the long way round
Looking
Not booking this hotel
Feels like I am in hell
words go a miss
The serpents tongue
I kiss
without fear
Feels like the devil is oh so near
I need to surrender
Don't have to be clever
If your ever bored trust in the lord

I am trying
To grasp
Feels like it's
Slipping past
Time is not mine
Content at the moment
Peace of mind
Where do you find
Lost in my mind
Ultimate sunshine
Forget drinking wine
Digging up brown
Look up don't look down
Come back around
Night watch out
I don't bite
But if pushed
I just might
Trying to live right
Before the dawn
On my experiences
I have drawn
Looking forward
To tomorrow morn

Even though I didn't
Do a thorough
Step 4 &5
God kept me
Long enough
To stay alive
And of course
There is remorse
Chasing a carrot
Around a race course
It was either get honest
And tell the truth
Or let my deceit
Hit the roof
To stumble
And get humble
There is a real trouble
Because my efforts
I need to redouble

Can you hold me
Can you show me
A better me
Trapped in thought
I have sought
Because I do seek
Don't want no beef
Looking for instant relief
It's the nature of the beast
For how long can
I hold my breath
The answer isn't suicide
from the light
I can't hide
Don't want to die
To be honest
All I do is admonish
Far from being an Adonis
Looking into the deep
Abyss
Don't stick in the knife
And twist
Need a lift
Need it quick

Newborn awakening
Innocent
Frustrating
Conscious
Inside of us
Breaking through
Freedom
For me and you
At a price
Locked in
Moments get spliced
Atoms nucleus
In everyone of us
Develope research
Articulate
Here on earth
All the time
I have been meaning
Make a new start
From a beginning
Poles apart
Common ground
I have found
Had to go around
And around
New reality
Forget depravity
Options
Have I really got them

Stop what your doing
This is a heist
In the middle of the night
Where do you stand
With Christ
Are you a man or are you mice
Take a chance
Roll of a dice
Sometimes I may think twice
There are flavours
Spice of life
Don't say just to please us
Where do you stand
With the Lord Jesus
Are you honest
A follower
Or a borrower
Do you believe in tomorrow
Do you confess give all to Jesus
Is it power that you lack
Do you know Jesus
Has your back

In my heart and soul
I hope I think I know
Just where I am going to go
And no it's not the south of Devon
I am talking about heaven
To be restored
No time to be bored
This promise can't be ignored
But needs to be explored
Jesus will greet me
He will meet me
When the time has passed
All the years come at last
I can rest in the knowledge
I will be one with the son
No more tears of frustration
Tears of joy
Adoration

As I fear
As I have done before
Of this life I want more
More laughter
More tears of joy
Even despair
I don't care
Better than what was on offer before
Just want more
Time to grieve
Time to let go
A seed of hope
In a desolate land
To get to hold your hand
To love
To grow
To articulate my feeling
To let you know
2017
What
Seeing is believing It remains to be seen
A human being
Time traveling
From this time to another year
And if your not quite clear
Start again
Another year

This is not a rehearsal
Thoughts universal
Everyone knows
But they are not willing to tell you
Every one is out to screw you
Wasted time
Is my crime
I can't get it back
Trace it
Get on track
The tide is against you
That is a fact
Another Chance not taken
This is heart breaking
Genuine not faking
In this moment
God give all that I need
Bring me up to speed I need
Educating
Your soul has vacating
Eyes are dead
Is it something I said

On this day
I have to say
If I don't try
I would surely die
If all was safe
And no risk
What if
I never put in
The action
There would be
just fear left
No satisfaction
All I am after
Is a little interaction
Something more than
I have already got
Am I asking for to much
Really it's not a lot

I gave up my vices
10 years ago
But there so
Much more to life
That I do not know
All I can be is open
And willing to give it a go
The seeds of hope
I am ready to sow
A crooked path
I have walked down
But I am free
I have turned it around
And this is what I see
A life lived in
Recovery

It's a possibility
No limits
Finally I can see
Dark cloud
Through the storm
I stand proud
Twisted thinking
Gone in a twinkling
What remains
I am sane
Playing the game
A serious one at that
Once in a while
I look back
To remind
But here and now
I find
To love you
To be kind
I don't mind
Just happy
Better than
Feeling crapy
Like a baby
Who has filled his nappy
Time took time
Let's not get snappy
As I look into your eyes
I feel something
Now that's a surprise
What the future holds
I can't prophesies

In life i am humble
In love I want more
Than a fumble
In a life full of grace
No longer do I stumble
If only I can see your face
The feeling I get from you
I can't replace
Recovery
No longer a disgrace
Once full of doubt
But had the courage
To ask you out
And if nothing
I can say
Let it be
Let go of the day

Being alive
Taking my time
Moments sublime
All at once
Consuming
Never out ruling
In this moment now
At this time of evening
Wow it's beyond believing
Quit done scheming
Reality
No more day dreaming
Icing on the cake
This is the cream
And living the dream
Alive now
I won't over look
Through every twist and cranny
Like reading a book
Foundations shook
Today I ain't no crook
A double take
A side look
like it's only
Just starting
In this moment
Celebrating
Culminating
At times a little frustrating
Real
in a nutshell
That's how I feel

Let's start at the beginning
And end at the end
If nothing more
I would like to be friends
Could it be true
I would like to get to know the real you
If you can bare the scars
On my wrists
I myself would take the risk
As we are on a journey
The road's never straight
On this path there are
Many twists
In life there are many desires
If I had you
I could resist
Because in this moment now
Your top of the list
Everything right now
Is as it should be
If I don't take this opportunity
I would miss
Seal our fate
With a kiss

Afraid
Afraid of what
Afraid of what I haven't got
Years of chasing the dragon
Misspent youth can you imagine
All the harm inside damaging
On the outside my habit
Was raging
My addict was caged in
Emotions roaring
Had to keep scoring
Till man it's so boring
Needed a little schooling
Had to learn quick
But every second
I hear the clock tick
Life slowed down
When i quit
Doing the brown
And in life what have I found
It's never to late
To turn it around

Can you sense
This feeling
It can be quite intense
No room now
For false pretence
Feelings pure
Can it endure
Would you like some more
If so pick me up from the floor
Because I've been down so long
Not quite sure what's going on
This feeling is instinct
On the verge
The start of the presipiss
At the start its rather
Hit and miss
Searching for the feeling
Which is bliss
It's time to rearrange
Time for change

I looked at you
You looked at me
Just maybe
There's a possibility
You spoke to me
With dignity
Then I would
Dare to see
Between us
Something
Could flourish
But if not
I won't go to pot
If this is just friendship
If that's all we got
It's enough
In fact quite a lot

I am sorry if I don't listen to your voice
is it because today
I think I choose
I think I have a choice
Well I believe it has been removed
If I love you do I have to prove
Acceptance is the key
Can your love
Set me free
Are you hurting
Feel like curtains
Nothing is so certain
Except love
Say for a child
Tender and mild
Love for an equal wild
Set fire to the night
Of these things I do not tire
I don't always get it right
Are you mentally undressing
Have you answered the question
Are you guessing
quit done stressing
In the end love from you is the best thing

I am inadequate
Can't seem to step up
People point out
My inconsistencies
I am in a prism
Not prison
Tripping on a thought
Into the bullshit
I have bought
Lack of understanding
Others are demanding
On my truth
I am standing
When others can't stand
Should I abandon
I need to work my program
Remember I am just as ill
I can feel
Touch there pain
In this fellowship
I will remain
Just to make it plain
How the next addict
Must be feeling
Pushing and pulling
in the same direction
From experience
I am not guessing

Every time I fear
I know you are near
Broken
But words softly spoken
I have a thought for a poem
Drenched in premeditation
Soaking with sweat
Evoking a feeling
Beaten
What ain't tied down
I am stealing
Are you done grieving
Cos I need to be given
To the living
Need to make a beginning
Some say live and let die
Why
I say love and be loved
love from the Lord
Never get boring
Never need to be scoring
My faith is soaring
I now have a power
Better than desire
A feeling sky high
I need to apply
Until the day
That I die

Mind is bending
Truly surrendering
Step one
Isn't much fun
Stuck in the pit
Man this is shit
I need to submit
Let go of it
Subject powerless
Wow what a mess
Need to confess
Get off my chest
And then
Step 10
Restored through inventory
Listen I will tell you My story
experience strength and hope
No longer shooting dope
But need a connection
Never rejecting
If you listen you can hear angels sing
For on the inside i am free
This is the good news
I bring

Help me
Because I have no vision
Done with starring at the
Television
Done with razors
Making an incision
It all started with
Making a decision
Volition is a beginning
Try to articulate
Explain describe
Elder statesman of the tribe
Like a shaman
Healing on the inside
I prayed for love
But you gave me rain
Indispensable
Water
You made the harvest
The power you harness
I did my darnedest
Self gone south
Going down
Beauty is an oasis

Stood in a bar
People so near
but so far
Took a taxi home by car
Dealt with thoughts
Some what out of sorts
Held it down
But now I have found
Never was easy
Took the long way round
Can anybody help me
Reach solid ground
In this theatre
On this stage
Seems this story
God has written every page
Me alone
With a phone
Like a dog with a bone
Sunny was the evening
Off the water the light was shimmering
Took a walk around coate water
Took in the scenery
Man it was beyond me
A sight to be seen
Although a little off beam

Time is an enemy of mine
Slipping past
I can't quite grasp
Want to steer it
In a direction
Seems I am always
Contemplating
Rarely do I put in the action
to make a connection
More or less stuck
In isolation
Can you free me
Can you see the real me
And not the person I appear to be
Confronting i am challenged
Rearranged malleable
Can't manage at all
But rather surrender it all
many times I will fall
Fail as well
Can you tell
My mood is heightened
A little bit frightened
Insecure I ask myself
Are you sure
Cause at the moment
I am on the floor

In this loo
Praying to you
That's all I can do
Need a little space
Time to contemplate
It's never to late
As I sit upon this throne
I realise I am not alone
Feel some thing better
Than I could manage
I can't manage my health
Cause when I am in doubt
Need to reach out
Weight barring down on me
Stuck so deep the malady
But when I am free
There's no holding me back
Power that is what I lack

Part of me is full of fear
Part of me wants to adhere
Part of me wants to run and hide
Part of me just can't define
Part of me is free
On the other hand
This life just has to be
Let go of fear
When you are near
Let go of rules
Because you rule
Surrender in the fact
When I am up against my back
Daily forgetting
It takes out the sting
I sing my soul of peace
A song of hope to last the day
I feel the breeze
You are part of me

Sigh
Don't want to let it
Pass me by
Emotions
But anger stops me
At the point I cry
A thousand thoughts
Can't discriminate
Or separate
Microism
One big cataclysm
Underlined rhythm
Synchronised
Look up to the sky's
And it's by no surprise
That I rely
On an inner resource
Most days divorced
From self pity
But can't help my mental health

Explain why I have to
Feel this pain
Feel like ripping out my veins
Gauging out my eyes
Carving my heart out
With a spoon
I feel full up
I have no room
It's coming around the bend soon
Or so I hope
Turned my back
On all the dope
In the darkness
I have to grope
The light that flickers
I need to stoke
would you ask
Because I need to say
Will love ever come my way
Because in this day I gave back
This is the area in life
That I lack

Feelings from the bottomless pit
Man I am deep in it
From feeling deep despair
Like who gives a shit
Haven't got the capacity
To care
When Alls lost
Can't argue the toss
Brother hood a grim jest
Really put to the test
I will ask God
He will know best
And although
From this cloud I will grow
Feels tough
Got to take the rough
With the smooth
Forgive me if I sound rude

She sat across the room
Before I was doomed
Now I assume
That because she
made me smile
And although I was
Apprehensive
Under no false pretences
Wasn't shy
But wasn't desperate
How it's gonna work out
I can't estimate
Is it too late
Could she be a lover
Or a mate
Just got to wait

Freedom
Over come
I am one
With an empty hand
Only by gods plan
Man I feel proud
Going to nymphs field in Stroud
Fellowship
That must not be missed
To drink or use again
You must be pissed
conscious contact
Once bankrupt
Please pray for me
Come to believe steps 1,2,3,

I wish I was a Christian
With nothing
On the inside missing
But that's not my mission
With hands that act
And an ear that listens
Because Christ has given
Although never been christened
Baptised in dirt
I gain my worth
Broken
Awoken
I used to toke and
Do all kinds of madness
Blasphemous
Turned away from the power
Of drink and drugs
Today I ain't no mug

Spirit in me
Give me
Clarity
Although ill
This is the deal
Walking up the hill
Without a drink hit or pill
Need to feel real
Sometimes surreal
Dream like
Not stuck in night
But drenched in light
The only thing that is right
Can't buy for a tenner
This feeling That is surrender

For those on the sly
Learning to just get by
Without getting high
To those trusting
Who are maladjusting
All the punks
Pimps whores
Thieves down right lowly
Recovery wasn't done in a day
It came slowly
To the misfit
When the instructions came out to life
We missed it
With my fellows
I have Mellowed
Once fearing
Now I am steering
To a life of joyousness
Welcome to the last stop on the bus

Need to face it
Need to embrace it
Make peace with it
Frustrated feeling
Discontent
Lament
Make some sense
Hurting
Pull the plug
Draw the curtains
I give up
But haven't given in
Nothing is making a beginning
Can we start again
Just want to be friends

The night is still
Cool air to breathe
Waiting for dawn
I yawn
Up again
No one answers the phone
Can't find a friend
Turn to Yahweh
He isn't to far away
Need
Want our God
cos now I am crawling the ceiling
Hallelujah
Never to far
Can't get to God
By driving a car
I wait for the sun
While praising the son

This writing poetry lark
Subject matter
Is quite dark
Something deep within
The nature of sin
Isn't pretty glamorous or exciting
Rather nail biting
Down right gritty
I take time
To write this ditty
Feeling explored
Can be shitty
A theme throughout
There is doubt
Discontent
My inner voice is screaming out
Would you contemplate
Is it a mistake
Could you conceive
This is how I came to believe

Run on instincts
Feeling is distinct
Thinking stinks
When will it cease
Never
That's the nature of the beast
Daily reprieve
Through the action of prayer
I come to believe
God you are the mender
With drink and drugs
I totally surrender
It doesn't discriminate
Nor age race and gender
With step one
A firm foundation
You can achieve meditation
If I am not adhering
Sanity disappearing
I think I broke the back
Next thing you know
I'll be smoking crack

I went to a meeting
And I did see
A lot of addicts
Suffer with the malady
One guy with a mental twist
One guy with scars
Around his wrist
One guy looked fine
But was out of time
A female crippled
With emotional pain
A couple of addicts
Restored and were sane
Some body talked about faith
And how they believed
Somebody picked up a key ring
And celebrated how they were clean
Every day I grow a little older
A little bit wiser another day sober
Every now and then
I get the feeling
and a reality
We all suffer the spiritual malady

In my opinion
I have been sinning
Right from the beginning
Can I get an amen
From a friend
Do I need to make amends
Saw a man in hospital detoxing
With this illness
He had been boxing
It won the fight
Down on his luck
I feel his pain
I did my cluck
now time to face up
Long way down
He must feel so small
So insignificant
Beginning to crawl
In this bad world
You can call
On me
When all is gone
I'll be the one
That's there I will care
When no one else's there

Heroin highly praised
It was my god
In those days
Heroin I did
My habit was well hid
Or so I thought
Was a buzz
Every time I bought
Just to hold it in my hand
With a needle in my vein
I felt like a god not a man
Every day I would inject
Even though I suspect
I was going down
Couldn't stop doing the brown
With a spoon and citric acid
Next time I would manage
Just need this hit now
Heroin is why I feel so low
Wanted to die in the end
with my friend smack
never thought I would get free
Thought I would die
With a needle in me

In the papers
Front pages covered
A heroin addict
Now recovered
Love from sisters and brothers
No more
Crawling the walls
Clucking
Sucking on a crack pipe
Is this how far I have fell
This existence feels like hell
The smell of smack
And a candle
No more veins
They have collapsed
No more
Don't want to relapse
Heroin is better than sex
10 years of sinking into an abyss
Now my recovery comes first
On my worst day of being sober
Is far better
Than my best day using
These are the facts
This is my conclusion

When I am focusing on you
I am diverted
Emancipation
Perverted
Eyes averted
When I am judging
Holding a grudge
Won't budge
When my thoughts
Pay rent in my head
I remember what my sponsor said
How free
do you want to be
In God there is a way
I no longer choose this day
The decision has been made
I have been saved
The right to choose has been waved

Basically we are all the same
In this drama
Playing this game
Me Tarzan
You Jane
Every one feels and bleeds
We are all planting seeds
For the future
We must nurture
Love your man
Don't try to understand
Your girl
We all fail
Don't know where we are going
But know where we have been
Brief intervals usually obscene
Sometimes egotistical and mean
But there runs a streak
High lowly and meek
On a journey we may seek
Don't try for an answer
Playing the game
Just take a chance
Sit this one out
Or join in the dance

On this path
Sometimes I feel the wrath
God will give me what I need
Not a second later
I am the instigator
Verbal resonator
Relationship complicator
I am not looking for a dream
I have it already
Taking everyday slow and steady
I never feel alone
God is with me in the room
Sorry if I don't measure up
God himself fills my cup
Sincerely
There is peace inside of me
I find rest
This is a drill
Not a test

I am overwhelmed
I need to calm down
By your glory
You are inside me
Presently pleasantly
To walk up a mountain
You need to take the
First step
I am growing
No longer socially inept
But there is a depth
The gift that keeps on giving
At the moment
I am really living
Something I have struck
It takes patience tolerance understanding
I don't believe it is luck
I remember the days
I used to be stuck
before asking questions
I would have struck
Today I am calm
Won't do you no harm
The Lord is my Shepard
Is my favourite psalm

In amongst the mess
I thought of you Jesus
I call you by name
Christ in me
When I was blind
Now I can see
You calmed the storm
Angels rejoiced
At the year you were born
You came my way
Yahweh
When the tunnel was at an end
In you I found a friend
In amongst the mess
I love you Jesus

If On the outside
You couldn't put on a plaster
If on the inside
It's a natural disaster
It's not top of my list
Ignorance is bliss
You can't see into my mind
For all you who are blind
The only thing you're aware of is the time
Yours not mine
Mental well being
Seeing is believing
If you can't see it
It's not really happening
On the outside I may look like
I am coping
It's astounding
Why would you think
My health is on the brink
Sober not taking a drink
I am aware of a great many things
And although on medication
My feelings are in freedom
I am not in incarceration
Looking at you I would never know
Please just talk to me
Like you would any one else
And yes in do suffer
With my mental health

When I am needing
Your the one
Who I believe in
Beaten into a state
Here at last
I wipe the slate
When it was almost to late
You are beyond my understanding
Couldn't plan for this
Not for all the riches
I would miss
all for your love
I want to caress
Sometimes there is great pain
It will come again
Turn it to an attribute embrace it
Peace in the moment
Own it
To be a little calmer
Live and let live
It's basic karma
What comes around
Goes around
This is what I have found
Not at all bound

It happens at times
Rightly or wrongly
I feel quite strongly
When I try to rest
Thoughts become a pest
Never a true word
Said in jest
Lord your putting me through tests
And if I could answer
I would say yes
Positive
Through negative
At its best
In this concrete field
I yield
I turn over
I surrender
Wish this feeling could last forever
Forfeit all
Here I call on your spirit
In my life want you in it
Like a chorus of angels
Forget the angles
Mental health
Now a wealth
Of knowledge
you never left my side
Today's trials
I can manage

Heart felt
dust myself down
And do up my belt
How many times do I have to learn
How many times
Am I going to get burned
With one foot in the past
And one foot in the future
On today
I am shitting
This life don't really matter
There is something greater
Far beyond comprehension
If things go wrong and don't work out
Or go my way
I will praise you any way
Beginning to end this short story
I praise your name
I give you the glory

Listen can you hear
listen it is oh so near
Distortion
No it is very clear
The stillness
Don't have to second guess
There is a quietness
Although there is no time to jest
But take it quite serious
A man with an outstretched hand
Hold on brother
I can understand like
No one else can
Would you care to look
In this big book
Can you surmise
Scales of prejudice
Fall from your eyes
A job done on the inside
Listen do you hear
That still soft voice
Did you wake up and choose
Because for me I had no choice
I has been removed
I can only win never lose

Eyelids drop
This is where this
evening stops
To sleep perchance to dream
In reality
There are seems
Pockets
Rocketed into the 4th dimension
Expanding
Can be very demanding
The cut off
The end and the start
In my dreams I play the part
Can separate
A time traveller
A measure of time
Disjointed
Never disappointed
A slip stream
What's your reality
Or do you just dream

In the dying of the light
Just around twilight
Feel out of sorts
May be its not my fault
Don't give it any more power
At this time of evening
At this hour
In the shadows I do cower
Start to suffer
Time to set it free
In step 3
Because it's to much for me
In darkness I can't see
In the light you can't hide
From the dark
Thoughts and feelings become
Rather stark

Without a purpose
Everything is just surplus
On show
My life is like a circus
Paranoid feelings
Need something
To believe in
Really seeing
Really living
Nothing in my hand
But I am giving
Don't know what's in store
life on life's terms
It's never a bore
But on the days
When it's more
More of a chore
I have found the key to open the door
And once more
I praise your name
Throughout the storm

I've become so numb
When I want to walk away
It isn't so much fun
I know I am not the only one
When I can't make sense
I feel so dumb
Turn my thoughts
To someone
so far I have come
But a long way to go
Because now I know
With this seed
It will grow
And if there's one thing I could say
Didn't have it my own way
Got tested
Was challenged
Had to put in the effort
some days with no comfort
Stripped bare to the Bare bones
Cocaine anonymous
Is where I found my home

This spiritual malady
Takes the best of me
Leaves me isolated
And in fear
Although people are near
Can't seem to think clear
Challenging not managing
Stuck
What the fuck
Trudging through the muck
It will knock you for six
Don't forget to duck
At least I am not doing a cluck
Injecting brown
Look up never down
May have taken
The Long way round

Inside I am screaming
Please stop this
Please Jesus
Taken from the top shelf
dealing with mental health
A thousand times
I ask to turn over
I know I have to surrender
Waves of paralysing fear
Within the malady appears
Most of my peers
End up mentally disturbed
Dead or locked away
I see it every day
God has a plan that
I don't understand
Another lost soul died today
I guess he tried
But couldn't find a better way

Stuck in the trip
Fear gripped
So I bit my bottom lip
Can anyone help me
Shelter me
I am astounded
Far from well rounded
Can't put in to words
Swindons back garden
My heart has hardened
Would you pardon
My ignorance
I am in a trance
Mad as a hatter
Sat in my underpants
It's a jungle out there
Or is it just potted plants
Need balance
Cos time has past
Every grain of sand in the hour glass

I met hope today
She smiles
And says anything
Is possible
Where once
I was hostile
Didn't think there
Would be another
Tomorrow
With elegance
Faith and grace
Truly put a smile
On my face
To think I was bankrupt
Just about to give up
Now hope lives in me
Only she can free me
I smiled
And in your eyes
I complied
Want to live not die
With hope by my side

When the poem doesn't rhyme
Everything takes too much time
When I am far from fine
It becomes appealing to do a line
Or drink wine
Or even have a hit
Man I feel shit
I have reached the limit
Full to the brim
A multitude of sins
Can some one just reach out
Do you know what I am talking about
Would it help if I had to shout
Screaming out
Tell me what are the positives again
Cause I can't see
Stuck in the malady
Soon this dark cloud will disappear
Soon I will think clear
And if not
If this is my lot
Then so be it

when i am falling
on you i will be calling
quit done stalling
sailing down the river
of hopelessness
you are the host
father son and holy ghost
want to live upmost
but then again
i surrender
contest i rest
tired from the struggle
in the boat of recovery
i am in the middle
no longer on the fiddle
in a canoe
who would have knew
i could feel brand spanking new
how this has been accomplish
i haven't got a clue

On the cusp
Of selfishness
Turn to you
Help you
Understand
I am just a man
Faults defects and shortcoming
I'll name the tune
That your humming
Stumbling through
A situation
Aiming for salvation
Clarity
All of me
Not just the bits that are pleasing
Seizing
A moment
Transparent
I see you in me
This is as should be
Please give me a slice of time
Another chance
To lay it on the line
Through the storm
There were times
Where the sun did shine

As I was observing
I saw you in a different light
Could it be wrong
Because it felt right
If I could let go
We just might
Share a moment
Felt like expressing
I know I am just guessing
Done with the messing
This feels like the right thing
To be happening
Friends
And I respect
You let me be me
And I you
At the moment
That's all I can do

Ask and you'll get
Today there are no regrets
Sometimes it's
Easy to forget
I used to be stinking and sodden
From the inside
I was rotten
The son
The only begotten
But only for a day
Can't live any other way
Want your embrace
There's no hurry
You set the pace
I am a human
In this race
What's my role
You moved the poles
Of this goal
What am I thinking
Would you like to know

Sometimes I forget who I am
Am I my name
No I am all in gods plan
Am I my voice nose or eyes
I am my personality
Is it a surprise
Am I my height weight or strength
I am my smile
I am my willingness
To go to any length
Am I my teeth hair
Colour of my skin
I am my determination
That I will win
Am I my intellect
Far much more than
I suspect
I am my spirit
That much I know
It's how I learn
I have to grow

Jesus I thank
How lowly I sank
Turned it over
In surrender
I stopped fussing and fighting
Senses heightened
In me and through me
Your love threw me
You loved me still
Can't imagine
What you went through for me
If I ever think
you don't give a toss
I am reminded of the cross
When it's all kicking off
When I feel all is lost
Turn to you in the moment
Your love is more than a component
I let god do what I can't do for my self
Freedom from addiction
A modern miracle of mental health

Once upon a time
I lost my mind
Today I have found
It took some time
I have searched
I did find
A power greater
Than my own mind
In my addiction
Moments sublime
Not all my experiences
Were bad
Cause these are
The experiences
I have had
And although sometimes
Were sad
Today I have gratitude
I am glad
I have taken the long way round
This is my experience
This is what I have found
Freedom from addiction
No longer bound

I looked in the mirror
And I did see
Someone who I didn't
Recognise starring at me
My eyes were dead
No light
Inside I had lost the fight
Drifting like drift wood
Couldn't see any thing worthwhile
Or good
Could not kick start
My wounded heart
Heroin tore it apart
Had to make a new beginning
Had to make a start
Turn over
To a new power
I looked and I did see
I am more than my addiction
More to me
But I needed help
More to me than my mental health
I looked at you
But you walked on by
Even so
I saw a spark
That could light up the dark

Can anyone tell
It's Andys daughter
Isobel
Even though
She only a kid
She 'may have scars
That are well hid
And she can teach
Many lessons
to give
With a smile you
Can't deny
Andy's child
Can't run and hide
From this joy
A dog is for life
Isobel is not a toy
Treat her with respect
Or she will strike
In full affect

Here I am I Am here
Nearly reached
The end of the year
A celebration we had
I myself stayed at my dads
Others in there homes
This is the experience I have had
The experience was good not bad
Sleeping on an air bed
Sonny had been sectioned
For the good I reckon
Jason faith and kin
Stayed at home
While my mind did roam
For those who haven't got a home
For those without a Christmas dinner
Jesus who died for the sinner
In the beginning
There was darkness
But then came a light
So that we might
Live and give to each other
Thank you for the gift of life
From my father and mother

You could stir with a stick
This atmosphere is thick
The malady so sick
The mind is an illusion
Tries to trick
Confusion
delusions
Mind abusing
Trust in it
It will fail
It will give out
For all the love in the world
It's not enough You call my bluff
Stuck in the rough
And thinking is on and off blinking
Reset the consciousness
Reset my soul
Is there an on off button
Feel stuck and sinking Fast
Oh well at the time it was a blast
Now in the malady
I have to bask

On my own
Writing this poem
A journal
On this journey
Come with me
Dealing with the internal
Inside out
But my outsides in
On this bed
Here I am lying
Need to get out what's going on
Deep in thought
Just another day
It won't be long
Surrender for this moment
Am I missing
A component
Trying to envision
I made a decision
In gods time not mine

To me this is a blessing
With the outcome
Don't want to be messing
And man this is the best thing
Couldn't plan or arrange
To me this isn't so strange
Have a new experience
No longer delinquents
Responsible
For me
this plan of recovery
Worked inside of me
Can't speak
I want to seek
Love from above
Or from within
On the inside
I am smiling

Valium
Come
Run
Not just one
Some
Stoned
The script I owned
Whites yellows and blues
These are my tools
The buzz ruled
It can't be fooled
Needles and spoons
Rushing
Feels like the second coming
God apart
In the morning
It is my start
The very beat of my heart

This existence
In my experience
Can be very distant
Long is the road
Heavy is the load
Long way to go
Till I can achieve
I really do believe
Are we spectators
Or participators
Going to get burned
Need to learn
It's something that I yearn
Everyone knows the sum
It's not for everyone
And again
I succumb
Done pretending
Truly surrendering

If you're disturbed
Talk to God
Or we can have words
Bring it back to the day
From using drink or drugs
There is another way
Come on what
Do you say
Are you in the blame game
Guilt remorse and shame
If you're willing
Quit done crawling
The ceiling
Live the dream
That's how I am dealing
Powerless I admit
I confess
It happens to to the best
And worst of us